ERZSÉBET SZŐNYI

MUSICAL

READING

AND

WRITING

PUPIL'S BOOK

VOLUME III

Lessons 47 to 57

Translated by Lili Halápy

Revised by Geoffry Russel–Smith

EDITIO MUSICA BUDAPEST

H-1370 Budapest, P.O.B. 322 • Tel.: (361) 236-1100 • Telefax: (361) 236-1101
E-mail: emb@emb.hu • Internet: http://www.emb.hu

"Let us find new paths if we want to make music available to all"
Zoltán KODÁLY

Zoltán Kodály conceived and realized the education of the young on the basis of the singing voice. Nevertheless he also kept in mind the education of those who were engaged in studying instruments. He himself had composed small pieces for beginners on the piano (Twenty-four Small Canons on Black Keys, Children's Dances) and he encouraged his disciples to compose exercises, solfeggios, instrumental tutors, and performance pieces for instruments in this spirit.

Thus, on the inspiration of the Kodály Method a series of tutors and performance pieces were written, as contributions to the new Hungarian method of musical education, opening new ways, and improving the general level of musical appreciation in consequence of which some remarkable results have already been achieved.

Our publications are compiled predominantly from Hungarian material: nevertheless Kodály's principles have been applied also to teaching music of non-Hungarian provenience.

The present volume is part of this series.

THE PUBLISHER

Printed in Hungary

Z. 6720

LESSON FORTY-SEVEN

1)

2)

The following $\frac{2}{4}$ tune should be sung with the above (a bar of $\frac{2}{4}$ is the equivalent to a ¢ bar of rhythm).

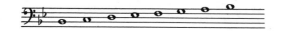

l m l | s   m | l l m l | s f m r | d

3/a)

I   II   III   IV   V   VI   VII   I

4

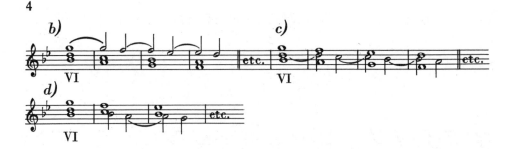

(Hungarian folksong)

(Hungarian folksong)

(Hungarian folksong)

7)

(Hungarian folksong)

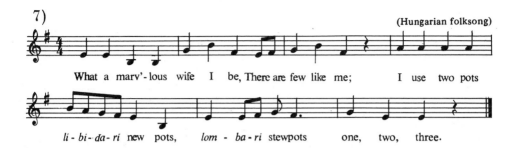

What a marv'-lous wife I be, There are few like me; I use two pots

li - bi - da - ri new pots, lom - ba - ri stewpots one, two, three.

8)

(Russian folksong)

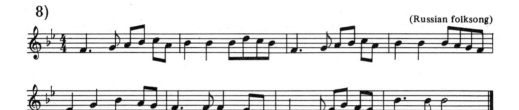

9)

(Hungarian folksong)

10)

(Purcell)

11) Giusto (Hungarian folksong)

Gaunt the si - lent for - est now that Sum - mer's done.

O how sad the branches when the leaves are gone

O how sad the branches when the leaves are gone

Sad - der still, the black - bird sing - ing all a - lone.

12) At a walking pace (Kodály)

Through the valleys,
So I left her,

Sway - ing with the rat - tle of the bu - sy train   O

Ne - ver could she love me with her sto - ny heart.   And

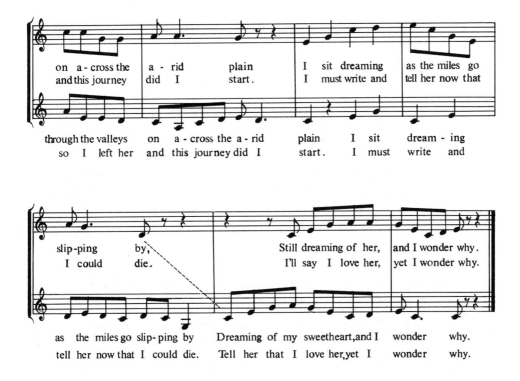

Homework: 1) practise, both by writing and recognition a) the intervals and b) the chords of B flat major; 2) write out and practise singing with the note-names the triads in D major in the broken chord patterns introduced in this lesson; 3) practise the same in B minor; 4) write out tunes Nos. 4 and 5 in the bass clef, and learn them by heart; 5) practise tune No. 10, singing one part and tapping the canon; 6) analyse this tune from the point of view of vertical intervals, and determine its compass; 7) practise tune No. 12, singing and tapping the two parts. Also analyse it from the point of view of form, intervals and structure.

LESSON FORTY-EIGHT

1/a)

lah_____ meh_____

b)

nah_____ meh_____ nah_____

2)

3)

(Hungarian folksong)

Seek the fair - est   of the las - ses

Deep a- mong the   de- wy gras - ses,

Pe - ter found her   where she tar - ried

And to mor - row   they'll be mar - ried.

Tap an ostinato to tune No. 7. The ostinato of the 3/4 time is:

and that of 2/4 time is:

8) Parlando (Hungarian folksong)

l₁ l₁ r m r d   l₁ l₁ r m   r d

l₁ l₁ r r s₁ s₁   d d r d   l₁ l₁

9)

(Hungarian folksong)

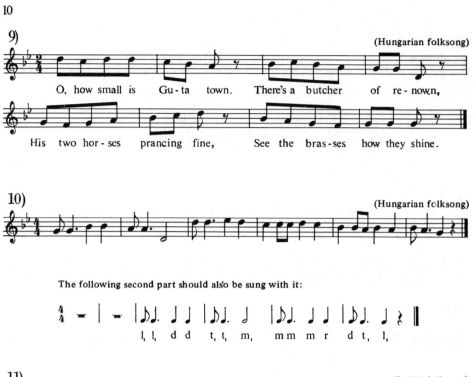

O, how small is Gu - ta town. There's a butcher of re - nown,

His two hor - ses prancing fine, See the bras - ses how they shine.

10)

(Hungarian folksong)

The following second part should also be sung with it:

l, l,   d   d   t, t,   m,   m m   m   r   d   t,   l,

11)

(Polish folksong)

12)

(Hungarian folksong)

s s s m   s m r d   m m   s   s s s m   s m r d   m r   d

m m m d   r d l, d   m r d   m m m m   r d r   d   l, l,   l,

This should also be practised in the form of a number of rhythm exercises. Ostinatos for the $\frac{4}{4}$ and $\frac{3}{4}$ bars should be found, e.g.: and Try clapping these while singing; tapping the complete rhythm while counting aloud, also adding the ostinato and first beat of the bar on triangle and drum respectively.

13) (Polish folksong)

14) (Beethoven)

15) (Kodály)

Slowly

Ga - ri - bal - di

Ga - ri - bal - di wore a lit - tle blue hat,

on his dappled horse sat. As he rode the peo - ple

Ga - ri - bal- di on his dappled horse sat. Peo - ple

16)

With gentle movement   (Kodály)

Where the | oats are | growing now, | There the | rows need | hoeing now,

Where the oats are growing now, There the rows need

Root out the | weeds that | tangle | them Lest they | choke and | strangle them

hoeing now, Root out the weeds that tangle them Lest they choke and strangle them.

Homework: 1) analyse the folksong on page 8; 2) write out all the triads of the G minor scale, and practise singing them to their names; 3) write out a list of the keys in which this chord occurs, together with the number of the degree in that key: ; 4) rewrite two of the dictation exercises in the bass clef, one of them with a one-flat key signature, and the other with a two-sharp key signature; 5) practise the two-part and canon tunes clapping the second part; 6) learn by heart tunes Nos. 7 and 13.

LESSON FORTY-NINE

Add a vocal part by singing a pentatonic scale to it, each note being one bar in length:

14

4)   (Russian folksong)

5)   (Hungarian folksong)

What you sel - ling, mar - ket la - dy?   Apples fine.
But how ma - ny for a pen - ny?   Eight or nine.

I should live to see the day she   makes it ten!   makes it ten!

6)   (Russian folksong)

7)   (Hungarian folksong)

m m l s   l   s m   l s l m   r   d l,

d r m l   s   m d   l m   r   d l, l,   l,

8)

The canon to No. 8 should also be tapped at one bar's distance, or it should be sung to the following tapped ostinato:

9) A (Hungarian folksong)

10)

11) Powerfully (Somerset folksong)

12) (A) (Hungarian folksong)

13) (Hungarian folksong)

Load the hay - cart, load it right up to the sky. Thorny brambles

hiding all a - round us lie. Have a care lest they should cut and

rip your skin; It is late and we must get the hay-crop in.

Practise particularly the sudden changes of clef. The following ostinato should also be tapped
to this melody: 3/4 ♩ ♫ ♩ | and 2/4 ♩. ♪|

14) Like a dance (Kodály)

O I've en - lis - ted, 'lis - ted for the ar - my life. Come, my
No, she an - swered, not for me the ar - my life; I can

O I've en - lis - ted, 'lis - ted for the ar - my life.
No, she an - swered, not for me the ar - my life;

sweet - heart, come and be a sol - dier's wife; Clean my
ne - ver e - ver be a sol - dier's wife. Such a

Come, my sweetheart, come and be a
I can ne - ver e - ver be a

Homework: 1) write tonal or real answers to the following melodies, indicating which you have chosen:

2) write out tune No. 7 with a two-flat key signature; 3) analyse the tunes from this lesson from all the points of view learned so far; 4) practise singing broken chords in various ways: on various degrees, with a common root, etc.; 5) learn by heart tunes Nos. 8, 9 and 11 (also practise tapping the canon to No. 8); 6) practise singing tune No. 14 while tapping the rhythm of the other part.

LESSON FIFTY

1)

2)

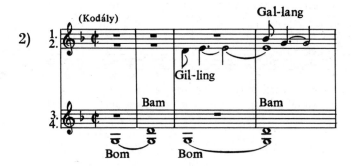

Section 1

Section 2

If possible, the pupils should conduct while tapping with the right hand. It is also easier to tap the rhythm while counting aloud.

7) (French folksong)

Clap a rhythm ostinato with it:

8) (French folksong)

9) (Hungarian folksong)

10) Andante (Scottish folksong)

11) (Beethoven)

12) (Russian folksong)

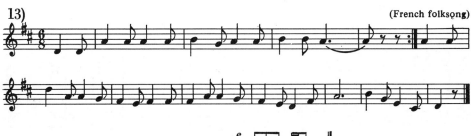

13) (French folksong)

Ostinato clapping:

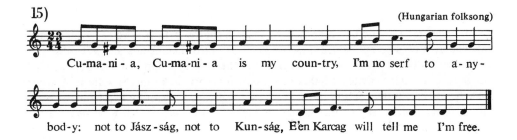

14) (Russian folksong)

15) (Hungarian folksong)

Cu-ma-ni-a, Cu-ma-ni-a is my coun-try, I'm no serf to a-ny-

bod-y: not to Jász-ság, not to Kun-ság, E'en Karcag will tell me I'm free.

16) Allegro (Beethoven)

17)

18)

Homework: 1) write out the whole of the bell chorus, with each voice having a separate line by way of completion; 2) practise singing all the other major scales learned so far; 3) devise further exercises using numerals for the singing of broken chords following the A major model; 4) write a rhythm exercise of four bars in $\frac{6}{8}$ time; 5) write an A major melody to the rhythm of the dictated rhythm exercise; 6) learn by heart tunes Nos. 6 and 9; 7) sing while tapping the rhythm of each part to tune No. 18; 8) analyse all the tunes from this lesson.

LESSON FIFTY-ONE

1)

The following $\frac{6}{8}$ melody, made up of broken chords, may also be added to the above, forming a four-part exercise.

d' s m d' l f   f l r' t r' s   s m s d' l l   s d' t d'

The following rhythm may also be tapped while singing the exercise.

Both the held chords and eighth-note passage can be used as vocal training, the vowels for the latter being treated thus:

 etc.

mah meh

2)

3)   (Chuwash folksong)

4)   (French folksong)

5)   (Hungarian folksong)

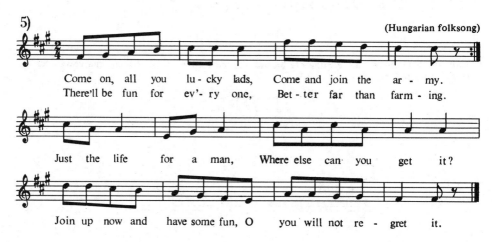

Come on, all you lu - cky lads, Come and join the ar - my.
There'll be fun for ev'- ry one, Bet - ter far than farm - ing.

Just the life for a man, Where else can you get it?

Join up now and have some fun, O you will not re - gret it.

6)   (Chuwash folksong)

This can also be used as a rhythm exercise.

7) Moderato (Bach)

8) (Hungarian folksong)

There's a stream in Os - to - pa - ny hey, my ro - ses hi -ya -hah

Rushes grow there for the tak-ing, hey, my ro-ses hi-ya -hah, Rushes grow there

for the tak-ing, Ripe for mats and basket making Hey, my ro-ses hi -ya -hah.

9) (French folksong)

10) (Slovakian folksong)

11) (Hungarian folksong)

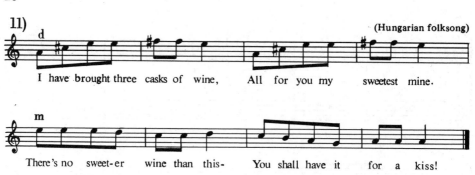

I have brought three casks of wine, All for you my sweetest mine.

There's no sweet-er wine than this- You shall have it for a kiss!

12) (Chuwash folksong)

13) (G. Rhaw)

14) (Chuwash folksong)

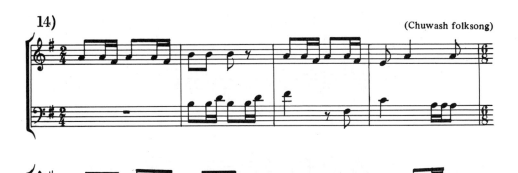

28

Homework: 1) analyse all the tunes from the lesson by way of revision; 2) write a detailed analysis of tune No. 14; 3) learn by heart tunes Nos. 5, 8 and 11; 4) devise an exercise involving broken chords based on the chords of the various degrees of F sharp minor using numerals, (see Lesson 42); 5) practise with particular care the exercises involving changing rhythms, clapping on the first beat of each bar, adding ostinatos, beating time with them etc.; 6) practise No. 14 singing one part and tapping the other; 7) refer to the work in Lesson 49 on tonal and real answers, and write either type to the following:

LESSON FIFTY-TWO

1)

Bel - la Ma - ry Jo - sie, Sa - rah

meh __ mah __ mah __ moh __

2)

3)

Clap and tap

4)

(French folksong)

5) Tranquillo   *pp*   (Kodály)

When as King Da- vid sore was af-flic - ted, By those he trusted   base-ly de-ser - ted,

In his great anger   bit - ter-ly griev- ing, Thus to Je-ho-vah   pray'd he with-in his   heart.

6) Rubato   (Hungarian folksong)

l l s s   s m s   l   s m   l   l l s l   s m s   m   r m   m

s   l m r   m m d r   m r d   l   s l m   m m r m   d l,   l,

7) Allegretto   (Hungarian folksong)

8) Leggiero   (Scottish folksong)

9) (Gretchaninov)

da Capo al Segno 𝄋

10) Allegro (Beethoven)

11) Ballade (Perrine) (French folksong)

12) (Armenian folksong)

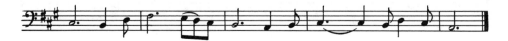

13) (Hungarian folksong)

14) Largo (Caldara)

15) Sadly and expressively (Kodály)

16)

(Purcell)

17)   (Haydn)

Homework: 1) write out a table of all the diminished and augmented intervals based on the note F; 2) practise singing with note-names the dictated sol-fa exercise in all the keys learned so far; 3) write a rhythm exercise of four bars in $\frac{9}{8}$; 4) write out tune No. 6 in the bass clef, beginning on C sharp: ; 5) learn by heart tunes Nos. 5 and 13; 6) practise the two-part and canon tunes, tapping the alternative part (in the case of the canon, tapping the second part).

LESSON FIFTY-THREE

1)

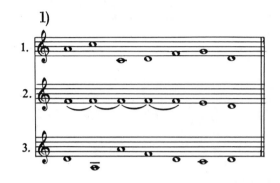

The following three-part ostinato rhythm in ¢ can be added:

2)

$\frac{3}{4}$ ♩ ♩ ♫ | $\frac{2}{4}$ ♫♩ | $\frac{3}{4}$ ♩ ♩ ♫ | $\frac{2}{4}$ ♫♩ | etc.

d s, r m   s t, d   r l, m f   l d r

3)

l, m ri m   d ta, l, | l, m ri m   d ta, l, | ......

d' si l |

d si l |........

4)

a)

b)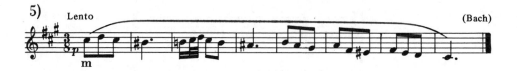

5) Lento   (Bach)

6) Andante cantabile con moto   (Beethoven)

7)   (Rózsavölgyi: Verbunk)

8)   d — m — ri — d — si$_,$ — l$_,$ — di — f — m — ta — fi — s — d

9)

(Hungarian folksong)

Full of fire is my bay mare. Bought her at the vill-age fair;

E - ven so, with her I'd part for the sake of my sweet heart.

10)

Allegretto

(Rumanian folksong)

This should also be sung accompanied by this ostinato:

11)

Andante

(Bach: Fugue)

12)

(Russian folksong)

13) Parlando   (Hungarian folksong)

Black the win - ter poplar,   Stark the win - ter scene love,

Stark the win - ter scene love.   But I'll be re - turn - ing

When it's leaves are green, love,   When it's leaves are green, love.

14)   (Karelian folksong)

15)

Poco rubato   (Hungarian folksong)

d r m m   s s l m   r r l,   d r m m   s s l m   r r l,

r r d d   m r d d   r m d   s m m m   d r r r   l, l,   l,

This can also be used as a rhythm exercise.

15/a)

This can be sung as an accompaniment to No. 15:

m r d d   d l, s, s,   r r d   l, l, m, m,   l, l, s, s,

s, s, l, l, s,   m, d,   m, r, r, s, s,   l, l,   l,

Homework: 1) practise the two three-flat scales in all the ways learned so far; 2) write out broken chords on all the degrees of E flat major and C minor, but varying the order of component notes (e.g. I. 1-3-5, II. 3-5-1 etc.); 3) practise singing the tunes involving thirty-second notes, tapping as an ostinato; 4) write a melody in E flat major to one of the dictated rhythm exercises; 5) practise singing the sequences employing identical sol-fa for each phrase to be found at the beginning of this lesson; 6) write out exercises 15 and 15/a below each other in two parts on two staves, the whole being in the key having a three-flat key signature; 7) learn by heart tunes Nos. 15 and 15/a (taken from Kodály: Bicinia Hungarica); 8) practise writing and singing tonal and real answers.

LESSON FIFTY-FOUR

1) Andante

2/a)

b)

3)

C min.:d   E min.:si   A : ti   E♭:fa   G: ta   si

A min.: si   f   F: ta

4)

Find and indicate the enharmonic pairs of the following intervals a) in words, b) in writing, c) in singing.

5)

To facilitate matters beat with your left palm the beginning of every ♩. value (thus there will be one beat for ⅜, two for 6/8 and three for 9/8).

6)

7)

(Hungarian folksong)

8) (Bach)

9) Allegro (Mozart)

10) (Bach)

11) (Hungarian folksong)

12) Moderato (Iusceanu)

13) Allegro  (Mozart)

p

14) (Hungarian folksong)

15) Poco lento (Bach)

Homework: 1) write a sequence similar to that at the beginning of the lesson, and practise singing it as shown; 2) determine and then write down the enharmonic notes of the degrees of the scale of E flat; 3) sing through slowly exercises to practise enharmonic intervals, taking great care over intonation; 4) tap with pencil and palm the $\frac{12}{8}$ rhythm exercise, including an exchange of parts; 5) learn by heart tunes Nos. 7 and 10; 6) practise No. 12 observing the dynamic and other indications.

LESSON FIFTY-FIVE

1)

C: 5   #1   b3   VII   1

2)

etc.

3)

4) Tap Clap 5/4   1 5   2 4   2   3 5

5) (Glinka)

(Hungarian folksong)

6/a)

d m   m   d   d l s s   m m m d r   m   r d   d

m m d r   d l, s,   d   m m d r   d l, l,   l,

(Hungarian folksong)

6/b)

m m m r   m m m r   s s l l   s m r d

s s l l   s m r d   s m r d   d l, l, l, l,

7)

8)   (Hungarian folksong)

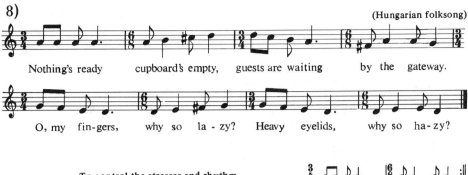

Nothing's ready   cupboard's empty,   guests are waiting   by the   gateway.

O, my   fin-gers,   why so   la - zy?   Heavy   eyelids,   why so ha - zy?

To control the stresses and rhythm,

this can be prac tised thus:

Tap

Clap

9)   Allegro   (A. Molnár)

1.

2.

3.

10)   (Russian folksong)

do

48

11) (Chuwash folksong)

12) Moderato (Hungarian folksong)

Come, sweet April, new life springing, o my flow-er, flow-er,

Birds are nesting fly-ing, sing-ing, o my flow-er, flow-er.

13) (Hungarian folksong)

5 5

I have lost my silk-en ker-chief on the way to mar-ket,

1 1

Has some-bod-y picked at up and put it in his pock-et?

14) (Chuwash folksong)

15)

Adagio

(Balakirev: Russian folksong)

16)

Slowly

(Kodály)

Aged   singer,   let   us   har - ken,   Sing your song thought skies may dark - en;

Fin - gers   stray - ing   On   your gitt - ern

Sing a - gain your fingers stray - ing   On   your gittern   id - ly play - ing.

id - ly   play - ing   From   your singing   let   us bor -

From your sing-ing   let   us bor - row

row   Courage   in   this   time of   sor - row.   Let   the songs that

Courage   in   this time of sor - row.   Let the songs that built our na - tion

built our na - tion Help us in this de- so- la - tion. From your singing

Help us in this de- so - la - tion. From your singing let us bor - row.

from your singing let us bor - row Hope, that we may face tomor - row.

Hope, that we may face tomor - row.

Homework: 1) write a rhythm exercise of four bars in $\frac{5}{4}$ time; 2) practise tapping this with a pencil in the right hand while tapping the bar division (2 plus 3, or 3 plus 2) with the left palm; 3) write out tune No. 8 at the pitch given, but with a key signature of four sharps; 4) practise the new scale in as many different ways as possible; 5) write broken chord sequences on the degrees of the E major and C sharp minor scales; 6) find *periods* among the tunes studied in previous lessons. (N.B. a great many will be found among the two-phrase songs which involve internal augmentation.); 7) write in E major an end-section to follow this beginning:

$\frac{6}{8}$ ♫♩ ♪♩ | ♫♩ ♪♩ | ♪♩ ♩. |
s m s m d   f m r m d   l l s

8) learn by heart tunes Nos. 9, 12 and 14. Include the text where this is given.

LESSON FIFTY-SIX

5)

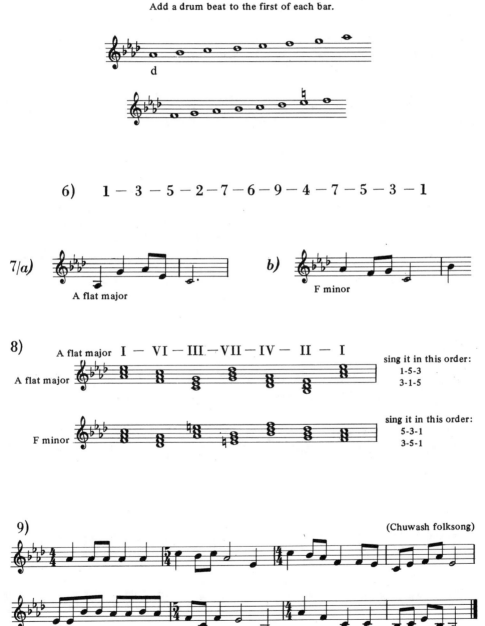

Add a drum beat to the first of each bar.

6)   1 — 3 — 5 — 2 — 7 — 6 — 9 — 4 — 7 — 5 — 3 — 1

7/a)   b)

A flat major   F minor

8)   A flat major   I — VI — III. — VII — IV — II — I

A flat major   sing it in this order:
                                                          1-5-3
                                                          3-1-5

F minor   sing it in this order:
                                                          5-3-1
                                                          3-5-1

9)   (Chuwash folksong)

10) Adagio cantabile (Beethoven)

11) Rubato (Hungarian folksong)

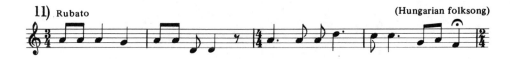

(Hungarian folksong)

12)

Ostinato

13) Presto (Haydn)

14) Tempo di mazurka (Polish folksong)

15) (Hungarian folksong)

Practise time No. 15 with ostinato clapping too:

16) (Cherubini)

17) Allegro giusto (Bach)

Homework: 1) write out in staff notation the $\frac{5}{8}$ tune given in sol-fa, beginning: 1-1-1-s, in a key with a four flat key signature; 2) practise clapping the rhythm exercise which involves changing time signatures. Count aloud while doing this, as in the lesson; 3) write chord exercises in the two newly learned keys; 4) learn tunes Nos. 9 and 15 by heart; 5) list the scales a single particular note occurs in, e.g. "G", and indicate which degree it is in the scales concerned.

LESSON FIFTY-SEVEN

1)

2)

3)

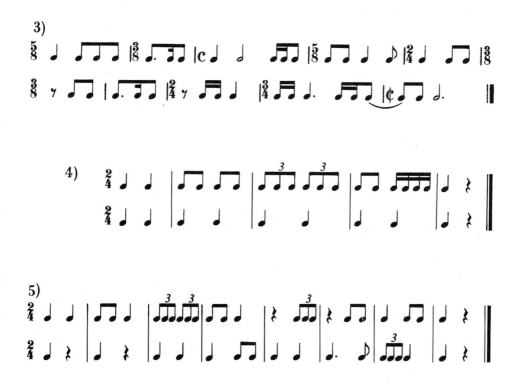

6)

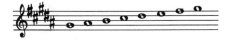

7)

8)

9)

Pe - ter is my po - ny, But I have no mo - ney

All his shoes need shoe-ing; It will be my ru - in!

The following ostinato should be tapped to this song:  etc.

10) Andante   (Tshaikovsky)

11) Compare:

12) Allegretto (Chinese folksong)

13) (Iusceanu)

14) (Mari folksong)

Was it dark that winter's night Long a-go when you bore me;

Black, without moon-light, Blacker than pitch and stor-my?

White as milk my brothers are, Born of fair-est wea-ther.

I am not as o-thers are: Black my skin, like lea-ther.

15)

This forms an accompaniment to tune No. 14 (Kodály)

m m d m r r r d r r m m m r l₁ m

d¹ m¹ r¹ l d¹ r¹ r s d¹ l s l m s l d¹

From the above the following rhythm exercise can be built:

16) (Stierlein)

17) (Evseyev)

Practise one of the vocal parts while tapping the other simultaneously.

18) Adagio (Kodály)

O the quivering flank, O the steaming side;

O the quivering flank, O, O the steam - ing

Homework: 1) practise one of the two-part rhythm exercises using both hands;
2) re-write the single-part melody taken down from dictation in the bass clef with a key-
signature of five sharps; 3) practise the B major and G sharp minor scales in the various
ways learned; 4) write answers to the following opening sections of a period:

l₁ d r m   l s l   t s l fi   m

5) find the intervals from the B major scale, write them down and practise singing them;
6) write down and sing the three-part chords of the two five-sharp scales; 7) analyse the
melodies from the lesson; how does the Chinese pentatonic tune No. 12 differ in structure
from the Hungarian pentatonic tunes; 8) write on two staves the two-part tune made from
Nos. 14 and 15 showing how they sound together; 9) learn by heart tunes Nos. 8 and 9.

ACKNOWLEDGEMENTS

The following copyright musical examples are included by kind
permission of the Publishers as shown:

1/ **BOOSEY & HAWKES MUSIC PUBLISHERS LTD., London**

A/ For all countries of the world except Hungary, Albania, Bulgaria,
Czechoslovakia, the German Democratic Republic, Poland and Rumania
(for these countries: EDITIO MUSICA BUDAPEST):

Bicinia Hungarica by Zoltán Kodály

Lesson 47, No. 12/		page 6
Lesson 48, No. 15/		page 11
No. 16/		page 12
Lesson 49, No. 14/		page 16
Lesson 50, No. 18/		page 22
Lesson 52, No. 15/		page 32
Lesson 54, No. 16/		page 44
Lesson 55, No. 16/		page 50
Lesson 56, No. 18/		page 56
Lesson 57, Nos. 15/ and 18/		page 61

B/ For all countries of the world except Hungary, Albania, Bulgaria,
China, Czechoslovakia, the German Democratic Republic, Jugoslavia,
Poland, Rumania and the Soviet Union (for these countries:
EDITIO MUSICA BUDAPEST):

Harangszó (Sound of Bells) choral work by Zoltán Kodály
Lesson 50, No. 2/   page 18

2/ **UNIVERSAL EDITION A.G., Wien** for all countries of the world:
Psalmus Hungaricus by Zoltán Kodály
Lesson 52, No. 5/   page 30

SOLFEGGIO / SZOLFÉZS

Works by Erzsébet Szőnyi / Szőnyi Erzsébet művei

–Biciniums
6648 I. – Japanese Songs / *Japán dalok*
6649 II. – American and Canadian Songs / *Amerikai és kanadai dalok*
8013 III. – American, Australian, Japanese, French and Transylvanian (Hungarian) Folksongs / *Amerikai, ausztrál, japán, francia és romániai magyar népdalok*
12372 IV. – French, English, Scottish, Danish, Norwegian and Swedish Folksongs / *Francia, angol, skót, dán, norvég és svéd népdalok*
12373 V. – Peruvian Folksongs / *Perui népdalok*
13306 VI. – Our Relatives and Acquaintances / *Rokonaink és ismerőseink népdalai*
– Musical Reading and Writing. Teachers' Books / *A zenei írás-olvasás módszertana. Tanári kézikönyvek*
1731 Vol. 1 (E)
13824 Vol. 1 (E)
1191 Vol. 2 (H)
1732 Vol. 3 (H)
5542 Final Volume (E, H)

– Musical Reading and Writing Exercise Books / *A zenei írás-olvasás gyakorló füzetei*

1953	Vol. 1	(H)
6718	Vol. 1	(E)
2063	Vol. 2	(H)
6719	Vol. 2	(E)
2064	Vol. 3	(H)
6720	Vol. 3	(E)
2065	Vol. 4	(H)
6721	Vol. 4	(E)
2066	Vol. 5	(H)
8630	Vol. 5	(E)
2067	Vol. 6	(H)
8631	Vol. 6	(E)
2068	Vol. 7	(H)
8632	Vol. 7	(E)
2069	Vol. 8	(H)
8633	Vol. 8	(E)

H = Hungarian edition
E = English edition